73124

920
BJA

Bjarkman, Peter C.

Top 10 baseball base
stealers

$18.42

DATE DUE	BORROWER'S NAME	ROOM NO.

73124

920
BJA

Bjarkman, Peter C.

Top 10 baseball base
stealers

SISKIYOU CO OFFICE ED/LIBRARY

925178 01842 31122B 32693E   002

TOP 10 BASEBALL BASE STEALERS

Peter C. Bjarkman

SPORTS TOP 10

ENSLOW PUBLISHERS, INC.

44 Fadem Rd.   P.O. Box 38
Box 699   Aldershot
Springfield, N.J. 07081   Hants GU12 6BP
U.S.A.   U.K.

Library of Congress Cataloging-in-Publication Data

Bjarkman, Peter C.
    Top 10 baseball base stealers / Peter C. Bjarkman.
        p. cm. — (Sports Top 10)
    Includes index.
    ISBN 0-89490-609-7
    1. Baseball players—United States—Biography—Juvenile
literature. [1. Baseball players.] I. Title. II. Title:
Top ten baseball base stealers. III. Series.
GV865.B58 1995
796.357′092′2—dc20
    [B]   94-45890
                                            CIP
                                             AC

Printed in the United States of America

10 9 8 7 6 5 4 3 2 1

Photo Credits: Gregory Drezdzon and the Cleveland Indians, p. 26; Los Angeles
Dodgers, pp. 43, 45; National Baseball Library & Archive, Cooperstown, N.Y., pp. 22,
25, 29, 37; Robert Constant, Passport Canada, p. 35; Transcendental Graphics, pp. 6,
9, 10, 13, 14, 17, 18, 21, 30, 33, 38, 41.

Cover Photo: Los Angeles Dodgers

Interior Design: Richard Stalzer

CONTENTS

Introduction

TODAY'S STYLE OF BASEBALL PLAY emphasizes foot speed and great athletic abilities. Above all, however, today's baseball excitement comes from the game's daring base runners. They steal bases and keep defensive players and pitchers in constant turmoil. Every successful team is built around a talented leadoff man like Rickey Henderson, Devon White, or Kenny Lofton, who will reach base regularly by stroking out base hits or coaxing pitchers for bases on balls and who will then move quickly into scoring position with baseball's most daring weapon—the stolen base.

Ty Cobb was the first and also the fiercest of these base path thieves. Cobb played in a long-forgotten era when baseball relied on a single runner reaching and then advancing around the base paths—often by his own daring maneuvers. Two runs was a big lead in Cobb's day, and one run, as often as not, was sufficient to win a tight ball game.

Although slugging was emphasized in the years just before and after World War II, two outstanding base runners brought new excitement to the game during the 1950s as well. Big league baseball's first African-American star, Jackie Robinson of the Brooklyn Dodgers, never stole large numbers of bases. But Robinson terrorized pitchers nonetheless by specializing in the rare and exciting steal of home plate. One of baseball's first Hispanic stars, Luís Aparicio from the South American nation of Venezuela, almost single-handedly made base stealing popular once again.

The stolen base today remains one of baseball's most exciting plays. The ten men featured in this book are among the game's greatest base-stealing artists from past and present eras of big league history. Each could dominate a ball game simply be getting onto the base paths and stealing second or third against the helpless opposition pitcher and catcher. Thus each was a superstar more for his base running than for any other feature of his game. These are the men who best represent baseball's most daring set of heroes—the kings of the base paths known as champion base stealers.

CAREER STATISTICS

Player		BA	G	AB	R	H	2B	3B	HR	RBI	SB
LUÍS APARICIO	*RS	.262	2,599	10,230	1,335	2,677	394	92	83	791	506
	*WS	.286	10	42	1	12	2	0	0	2	1
LOU BROCK	*RS	.293	2,616	10,332	1,610	3,023	486	141	149	900	938
	*WS	.391	21	87	16	34	7	2	4	13	14
TY COBB	*RS	.366	3,035	11,434	2,246	4,189	724	295	117	1,937	891
	*WS	.262	17	65	7	17	4	1	0	11	4
EDDIE COLLINS	*RS	.333	2,826	9,949	1,821	3,312	438	186	47	1,300	744
	*WS	.328	34	128	20	42	7	2	0	11	14
RICKEY HENDERSON	*RS	.289	2,080	7,656	1,652	2,216	364	56	226	804	1,117
	*WS	.412	8	34	6	14	3	2	2	4	6
KENNY LOFTON	*RS	.312	428	1,678	326	524	76	25	18	141	198
	*WS	None									
JOE MORGAN	*RS	.271	2,649	9,277	1,650	2,517	449	96	268	1,133	689
	*WS	.235	23	85	14	20	4	2	3	8	7
TIM RAINES	*RS	.296	1,920	7,264	1,293	2,152	346	105	134	762	764
	*WS	None									
JACKIE ROBINSON	*RS	.311	1,382	4,877	947	1,518	273	54	137	734	197
	*WS	.234	38	137	22	32	7	1	2	12	6
MAURY WILLS	*RS	.281	1,942	7,588	1,067	2,134	177	71	20	458	586
	*WS	.244	21	78	6	19	3	0	0	4	6

*RS = Regular Season
*WS = World Series

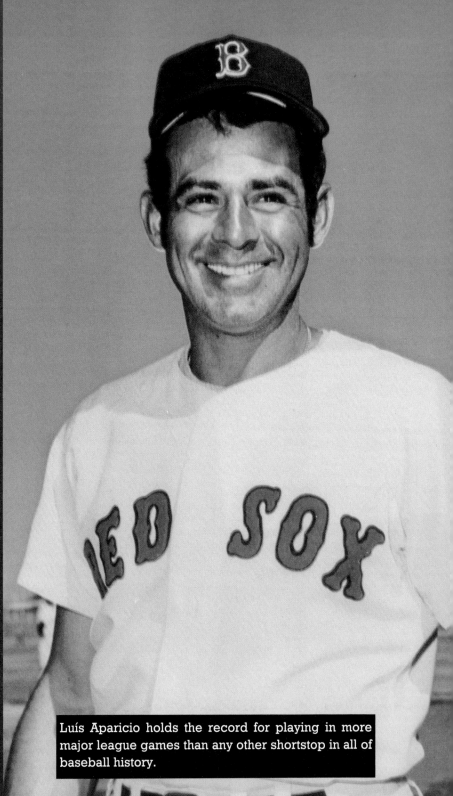

LUÍS APARICIO

Luís Aparicio holds the record for playing in more major league games than any other shortstop in all of baseball history.

BASEBALL INDEED HAS MANY FORGOTTEN pioneers, but most come from the dim and distant decades of the game's nineteenth-century beginnings.

Yet when it comes to those talented speedsters who influence the outcome of ball games with their daring base running, no modern-day star is perhaps more unjustly forgotten or more widely underappreciated than the talented Hall-of-Fame shortstop who hailed from the Caribbean nation of Venezuela. Few Chicago White Sox fans from the decade of the late 1950s and early 1960s can ever, of course, altogether forget flashy Luís Aparicio. It was the tiny but colorful Aparicio, after all, who teamed with second sacker Nellie Fox to provide one of the slickest-fielding double play combinations in diamond history. Aparicio does indeed own a measure of fame as the man who played in more major league games than any other shortstop before or since.

But when it comes to recording the game's greatest base stealers, few today remember that it was also Aparicio—and not Cobb, Wills, Brock, or Henderson—who is most responsible for reinventing the stolen base as one of baseball's greatest secret weapons. Aparicio's base-stealing totals were never large. But with the quick Aparicio running wild on the bases and also guarding the infield, Chicago built a new type of pennant-winning team.

In his own nation of Venezuela, Luís Aparicio is far from a forgotten hero. Young Aparicio played the game on the sandlots of his home in the coastal city of Maracaibo, all the while dreaming of someday making it to the majors in the footsteps of his idol, the older Alfonso "Chico" Carrasquel.

That dream would be fulfilled when the speedy Aparicio worked his way through the farm system of the same Chicago team and soon replaced his hero as the starting White Sox shortstop. Aparicio would inherit another role from his countryman as well, that of the most popular White Sox player of the 1950s.

The first Venezuelan baseball hero, Carrasquel, earned his smaller measure of fame with his fancy glovework. Aparicio—also an excellent fielder—would also earn his reputation with his fancy footwork on the base paths. "Little Looie," as Chicago fans knew him, would quickly compile a base-stealing record matched by none among the game's greatest base-running artists. Maury Wills has often been given most of the credit for reviving the base-running art for the National League Dodgers in the early 1960s.[1] But by then Aparicio had already been working his magic against American League pitchers for more than a half-dozen seasons.

Beginning with his rookie season of 1956, Aparicio would reign as league base-stealing champion for nine consecutive seasons, each of his first nine seasons in the major leagues. No base runner before or since has registered such a feat. As modern baseball's first great base stealer, Ty Cobb had won only six league titles. Rickey Henderson would one day own eleven base-stealing crowns, but his consecutive titles would never stretch beyond seven. Vince Coleman would also one day dominate all base stealers in the National League as Aparicio had once done in the junior circuit, but Coleman's own string of titles at the beginning of his career would stop at six. When it came to consistency and lasting domination, Luís Aparicio would remain unchallenged as baseball's longest-lasting base-stealing champion of all-time.

LUÍS APARICIO

BORN: April 29, 1934, Maracaibo, Venezuela.

CAREER: 1956–1973.

TEAMS: Chicago White Sox, Baltimore Orioles, Boston Red Sox.

POSITION: Shortstop.

AWARDS AND ACHIEVEMENTS: American League Rookie of the Year, 1956.

American League Stolen Base Champion, 1956–1964.

Gold Glove Shortstop, 1958–1962, 1964, 1966, 1968, 1970.

American League Leader in Fielding Percentage for Shortstops, 1959–1966.

Baseball Hall of Fame, Elected 1984.

Beginning with his rookie year, Luís Aparicio was the league base-stealing champion for nine consecutive seasons.

LOU BROCK

Lou Brock dominated both the 1967 and 1968 World Series—stealing seven bases in each.

IT WAS THE OPENING GAME of the 1967 World Series and the St. Louis Cardinals were heavy favorites to defeat their American League rivals, the Boston Red Sox. The Cardinals appeared to have the superior lineup of recognized All-Star players. Ace pitcher Bob Gibson headed up the mound staff, while veteran first baseman Orlando Cepeda provided the heavy hitting and was the senior circuit's RBI champion. Fleet outfielder Lou Brock had paced the league in stolen bases for the second straight year and led all rival players in runs scored as well, while collecting more than 200 base hits. Knowledgeable baseball people and fans just about everywhere, except in Boston, were betting heavily on the powerhouse National League team from St. Louis.

But the series soon proved a lot closer than expected, and the hitting of Boston's Triple Crown-winner Carl Yastrzemski along with the pitching of Boston ace Jim Lonborg would eventually force seven hard-fought games to decide the championship. No single game in this classic series would prove more dramatic or more vital than the one that St. Louis captured in Boston on the opening day of championship play. Cardinal ace Gibson battled unheralded José Santiago of Boston in a marvelous pitching duel that stood tied at one apiece after six innings. Boston's only run had come on a surprise homer by Boston hurler Santiago.

Then, in the seventh inning, the tide turned slightly when Lou Brock singled to open the frame. The speedy outfielder next stole second base, as he had so often done all season. That single stolen base may indeed have been the most important moment of the memorable series. Two usually harmless ground ball outs would first move Brock on to third and then allow him to score a run that proved to be the game winner. After six more tense contests, Brock's opening game-winning run would eventually prove to be the slim margin of difference that measured victory for the Cardinals.

The Cardinals would be back in the Fall Classic to defend their title against the powerful Detroit Tigers one season later. Lou Brock would also be back to prove that his 1967 World Series heroics had been anything but a fluke. For in the 1968 World Series, no one owned the diamond more than Lou Brock. In fact, few players have ever dominated the Fall Classic for two straight years the way Lou Brock once did. The long-legged lefty hitter had already stolen 7 bases during the 1967 Classic, and he would now match that figure with 7 more in 1968. Brock also batted over .400 both years, connecting for a sterling .414 average against Boston and then a .464 average versus Detroit.

This second time around Brock's daring base running and solid hitting would prove insufficient as the Cardinals were bested in the seventh game by a Tigers team that had even more pitching and hitting than the powerful National Leaguers. Yet the World Series legacy of the St. Louis outfielder would remain unchallenged for years to come. Lou Brock is still the World Series career leader for stolen bases and still has the second highest lifetime series batting average. Eddie Collins of the World War I-era Athletics and White Sox once stole the same number of bases in series play, but it took Collins 6 different World Series and 34 games to achieve the same number of stolen bases as Brock. When it came to the clutch championship games, Lou Brock was a true base-running champion.

When he retired he was baseball's greatest base-stealing king ever. Only Rickey Henderson would eventually dim the marks set by Lou Brock of the St. Louis Cardinals.

LOU BROCK

BORN: June 18, 1939, El Dorado, Arkansas.

CAREER: 1961–1979.

TEAMS: Chicago Cubs, St. Louis Cardinals.

POSITION: Outfielder.

AWARDS AND ACHIEVEMENTS: National League Stolen Base Champion,
1966–1969, 1971–1974.

National League Leader in Runs Scored, 1967, 1971.

National League Leader in Doubles and Triples, 1968.

Baseball Hall of Fame, Elected 1985.

Lou Brock remained baseball's base-stealing leader for years.
It was not until Rickey Henderson came along that Brock's records
were beaten.

TY COBB

Known as the fiercest competitor ever on the diamond, Cobb spent twenty-four years playing baseball in the major leagues.

Ty Co

TYRUS RAYMOND COBB WAS THE FIERCEST competitor ever seen on a professional or amateur baseball diamond. Cobb, who starred with the Detroit Tigers during the first two decades of the present century, was also the meanest player who ever had an impact on the game. His biographers tell stories of Ty Cobb sitting on the dugout steps before games and filing his already sharp spikes to intimidate opposing players.[1] The truth is that Cobb apparently only sharpened his spikes once in public, and then it was more for show than for serious intimidation.

But intimidation was indeed an important part of Cobb's game, even if legend often exaggerated his vicious intentions. Once Cobb's spikes were strapped to his feet, he did not hesitate to use them to scare any enemy infielder from defending the second or third base bags. Many infielders and catchers therefore felt the pain of Cobb's metal spikes as he slid into second, swiped third with another devastating steal, then dashed home with a crucial game-winning run.

But Cobb's meanness came not only from his sour personality and his excessive will to win. This was also one of baseball's smartest players ever to lace on a pair of baseball shoes or pick up a wooden bat. He somehow knew almost by instinct how to gain an important edge over his rivals. Cobb enjoyed great success at the plate, for example, against one of the league's most fearsome pitchers, fastballing Walter Johnson. Cobb knew that the mild-mannered and gentlemanly Johnson had a fear of maiming opposing hitters with his deadly fastball. So Cobb took full advantage and stood directly on top of the plate, his spikes against the inside edge of the batter's box and his body leaning out into the strike zone.[2] This was one of the many ways that Ty Cobb intimidated and defeated his opponents.

Ty Cobb spent his twenty-four years in the big leagues intimidating his rivals with two lethal weapons. One was his bat, for Cobb was the greatest singles hitter the game has ever known. Twelve times he won batting titles, and nine of these came in a row. Sixty-five years after his retirement from the sport, Cobb still ranks as the greatest hitter in history with a lifetime batting average of .366, eight points higher than that of nearest rival, Rogers Hornsby. Only Pete Rose has passed Cobb as baseball's all-time leader in base hits; no one has yet matched his record of twelve league batting championships; and only Rogers Hornsby has equaled his mark of hitting over .400 three different times in this century.

But even more threatening were Cobb's feet. Once on base—the seemingly inevitable result of his batting skill—the fearless Detroit outfielder was the most reckless and daring base runner the sport has ever known. Over his long career, he stole nearly 900 bases, a record that was once considered to be truly unbreakable. Only Lou Brock and Rickey Henderson have yet reached Ty Cobb's lifetime base-stealing totals.

The competitive nature of Ty Cobb won many baseball games for the Tigers and a long list of individual batting and base-running titles for the "Georgia Peach" himself. But his excessively vicious style made many enemies. Cobb was perhaps the most universally hated of all ballplayers. His rivals and even his teammates may have disliked the man personally; however, none ever questioned his abilities as baseball's first great base stealer. When the Hall of Fame's very first elections were held in 1936, Ty Cobb stood next to Babe Ruth, Honus Wagner, Walter Johnson, and Christy Mathewson as one of the first five greats selected.

TY COBB

BORN: December 18, 1886, Narrows, Georgia.

CAREER: 1905–1928.

TEAMS: Detroit Tigers, Philadelphia Athletics.

POSITION: Outfielder.

DIED: July 17, 1961, Atlanta, Georgia.

AWARDS AND ACHIEVEMENTS: American League Most Valuable Player, 1911.

American League Stolen Base Champion, 1907, 1909, 1911, 1915–1917.

American League Batting Champion, 1907–1915, 1917–1919.

American League Leader in Base Hits, 1907–1909, 1911–1912, 1915, 1917, 1919.

All-Time Career Leader in Runs (2,246) and Batting Average (.366).

Baseball Hall of Fame, Elected 1936.

Cobb stole nearly 900 bases during his long career, making him baseball's first great base stealer.

EDDIE COLLINS

Eddie Collins was skilled at reading other teams' signs and signals. He took advantage of this skill in order to steal bases more easily.

EDDIE COLLINS

IF THERE IS A FORGOTTEN HERO of baseball history, it is Eddie Collins, longtime second base star with the Connie Mack Athletics of the 1910s and the Charlie Comiskey White Sox of the 1920s. Collins had one of the longest and most productive careers of any player to play the game—batting .333 and recording 3,312 base hits, the eighth best all-time career mark. He was also one of the most versatile all-around ballplayers ever to set foot on a baseball diamond. His career spanned the first three decades of the twentieth century, and he was a star at two different styles of play in two different playing eras. First he excelled in the pitching-dominated age of Ty Cobb, immediately before World War I. Then he adjusted to the new style of free-swinging in the lively hitting era of Babe Ruth and remained a star with the White Sox throughout the 1920s as well.

For those who played both with and against him, he was known as "Cocky Collins" for his confident style of play. He was extremely confident in his abilities—abilities so great that his confidence was never seen by teammates and rivals as conceit. Collins simply believed he was one of the best men on the diamond.

During the very best years of his career, Collins was an expert hitter, but he won no batting titles. Ty Cobb, George Sisler, and Joe Jackson—men who all once hit .400—were all playing in that same era. The batting title usually went to Cobb, who also had a reputation as the game's best base runner and base stealer. But Eddie Collins never took a back seat to Ty Cobb when it came to base running. Four times Collins led Cobb and the rest of the league in steals, and three straight years (1912–1914) he was also a league leader in scoring the most runs. In the end, the 744 career stolen bases by Collins come close to those of Ty Cobb.

Collins was also a brilliant bunter in an age that utilized the bunt as a major weapon. He was a superb slashing hit-and-run man who played the "one-base-at-a-time" game to near perfection. He was also a skilled stealer of opposition coaching signs and signals as well as of enemy bases. Few matched his knowledge of strategy either. Most of all he was a daring and clever base runner who perfected both the art of getting on base and the art of getting back to home plate.

Eddie Collins's star-studded career with the Philadelphia teams of manager Connie Mack came to an end when the tight-fisted Mack disbanded his championship club after the 1914 season and sold his star second baseman to the White Sox. With his new club, Collins would soon star in the 1917 World Series. In that series, he would score a key run that resulted from the type of expert base running that had come to distinguish his brilliant career. The Sox were rallying in the fourth inning of the sixth game with the series squarely on the line. Collins had been caught in a rundown between home and third and danced away from the infielders chasing him so that two other White Sox runners could advance into scoring position. Suddenly, the always-alert Collins saw that the plate had been left uncovered. He skillfully dashed around a startled Giants catcher who had just released the ball to third baseman Heinie Zimmerman. With Zimmerman hopelessly chasing behind him, Collins dashed homeward with the dramatic run that led to the series victory.

Collins's famous dash to the plate was the only time that a runner avoiding a rundown directly resulted in a World Series victory. Collins's daring run through the amazed Giants infield was thus perhaps the most important single base-running maneuver in all of baseball history.

EDDIE COLLINS

BORN: Birthdate: May 2, 1887, Millerton, New York.

CAREER: 1906–1930.

TEAMS: Philadelphia Athletics, Chicago White Sox.

POSITION: Second Baseman.

DIED: March 24, 1951, Boston, Massachusetts.

AWARDS AND ACHIEVEMENTS: American League Most Valuable Player, 1914.

American League Stolen Base Champion, 1910, 1919, 1923–1924.

American League Leader in Runs Scored, 1912–1914.

American League Leader in Fielding Percentage for Second Basemen, 1909–1910, 1914–1916, 1920–1922, 1924.

Baseball Hall of Fame, Elected 1939.

"Cocky Collins" stole home, scoring a dramatic run in the 1917 World Series that led to the series victory.

RICKEY HENDERSON

Rickey Henderson was the first major league player to ever slug 20 homers and steal more than 70 bases in a single season.

RICKEY HENDERSON

THE OAKLAND'S ATHLETICS AND TORONTO'S Blue Jays were locked in a tight play-off struggle for baseball's American League championship of 1989. The winner of the best-of-seven play-off would advance to the World Series. Late in the important first game, Rickey Henderson of Oakland drew a base on balls. Moments later Henderson slid hard into Blue Jays' second baseman Nelson Liriano, breaking up a certain double play and sparking a game-winning rally for the Athletics.

Henderson's base-running skill has established him as one of today's brightest big league stars. As important as he was to Oakland's pennant hopes in October 1989, however, Henderson's fame did not come from a single series or even from a single season. It came instead from a full decade of speed and daring along the base paths. As the first big leaguer ever to slug 20 homers and steal more than 70 bases in the same season, Rickey Henderson has wasted little time in establishing himself as the ultimate lead-off hitter in all of baseball history.[1]

Henderson became an instant star with the Oakland Athletics in the late 1970s. He first stunned the baseball world when he stole 100 bases in only his second year of big league play. Later he outdid Cobb, Wills, and Brock all at once during a marvelous 1982 performance in which he pushed the single-season record for steals to an unthinkable 130, a dozen more than Lou Brock's highest total.

Soon Rickey Henderson was terrorizing American League pitchers and catchers from a new home in New York's Yankee Stadium. In a stunning December 1984 trade, owner George Steinbrenner's Yankees had given up five players, including future pitching star José Rijo, just to obtain the talented base stealer from Oakland. For a while it looked like one of the best trades that the proud Yankee franchise had ever made. Almost immediately Henderson began to pay huge dividends for the New York team, and most of those payoffs had to do with his terrific base-running skills. During his first New York season, Henderson became the first American League player ever to combine 20 homers with 50 stolen bases in a single summer—he actually slugged 24 round-trippers and swiped 80 enemy bases. Again in 1986 he repeated the same feat, this time recording 28 homers and 87 steals. It was at Yankee Stadium that the speedster also established himself as the heaviest-hitting leadoff man in baseball history, soon topping Bobby Bonds's record for leading off ball games with home runs. But a series of injuries in the form of pulled hamstring muscles and sprained ankles began to slow the speedster in the late 1980s. Eventually club owner Steinbrenner decided that he was no longer getting full value out of his top outfield star.

During the 1989 season, Rickey Henderson was traded back to his first team, the Athletics, and thus returned to his hometown of Oakland. By season's end, he would lead the West Coast team to its second of three straight World Series appearances. But despite these team glories in Oakland, Henderson also had an important personal milestone yet to reach. That milestone was achieved on May 1, 1991, when Rickey Henderson stole his 939th base against his former Yankee teammates.

Henderson had now passed another of Lou Brock's records, but he was humble when he recalled the joy of his achievement. "My first reaction was to hug Lou," Henderson remembers, "since he had given me so much inspiration throughout my career."[2] Rickey Henderson was now baseball's all-time stolen base champion.

RICKEY HENDERSON

BORN: December 25, 1958, Chicago, Illinois.

CAREER: 1979–

TEAMS: Oakland Athletics, New York Yankees, Toronto Blue Jays.

POSITION: Outfielder.

AWARDS AND ACHIEVEMENTS: American League Most Valuable
     Player, 1990.

     American League Stolen Base Champion, 1980–1986,
     1988–1991.

     American League Leader in Runs Scored, 1981, 1985–1986,
     1989–1990.

     American League Leader in Base Hits, 1981.

     Gold Glove Outfielder, 1981.

     American League Championship Series Most Valuable
     Player, 1989.

     All-Time Leader in Stolen Bases for Single Season (130 in
     1982) and Career.

In 1991, Henderson stole his 939th base, making him baseball's
all-time stolen base champion.

KENNY LOFTON

The first rookie since Luís Aparicio to lead the league in the base-running category, Kenny Lofton is a major threat to opposing teams.

KENNY LOFTON HAD FIRST BEEN noticed by pro-basketball scouts when he performed as a talented "sixth man" off the bench on the Arizona team that advanced all the way to the NCAA Final Four in the spring of 1988. Once inserted in the Wildcats starting lineup a season later, Lofton proved to be not only a skilled offensive performer but one of the quickest defenders in the Pac-10 Conference. With hands almost as quick as his feet, Ken Lofton made life miserable for all of the opposition backcourt men he guarded. The specialty of this Wildcat guard was the stolen pass or dribble, and by the time he closed his college basketball career, Lofton owned the Arizona career record for steals, along with the single-season record as well.

Although he did not play varsity baseball at Arizona until late into his junior year, Kenny Lofton had set his private dreams on the major league diamonds and not on the NBA arenas. The Houston Astros recognized Lofton's baseball potential, and only a few weeks after the closing of his basketball career in the spring of 1989, Lofton was already patrolling the outfield for the Astros Class A minor league club at Auburn in the New York-Penn League. Lofton suddenly found himself not only living out his personal baseball dream but also learning how to properly play the game that had not received much of his attention since high school days. Kenny Lofton proved to be a quick learner indeed.

Only three summers later the former basketball ace was testing his mettle as an American League baseball rookie with the big-league Cleveland Indians. What a sensational rookie he became. A .285 batting average along with brilliant defensive outfield play was enough to earn runner-up status in the race for 1992 American League Rookie of the Year. It was as a base runner that Lofton early and dramatically made his most memorable mark. Once again it was the steal that would become Lofton's special calling card. But this time the Indiana speedster was stealing bases, not enemy passes or the opposition's errant dribbles.

By midsummer 1992, American League hurlers had a new base-stealing threat to worry about, one who appeared every bit as dangerous as now fading veterans like Rickey Henderson, Vince Coleman, and Rock Raines. The rookie threat from Cleveland was suddenly working his way regularly onto the base paths as one of the outstanding young leadoff hitters in the league. Once entrenched on the bases, he was pilfering sacks at a record pace. Lofton would lead the junior circuit in stolen bases that summer with 66 in only 78 attempts, meaning that he was successful an outstanding 85 percent of the time. Lofton had shattered the American League rookie record for steals as he surpassed the former mark of 50 by John Cangelosi with more than a month remaining in the season. He was the first rookie to lead the league in the important base-running category since Hall-of-Famer Luís Aparicio did it way back in 1956. Also, he was the first Clevelander to earn the honor since George Case had turned the trick a full decade before Aparicio.

Kenny Lofton of the Cleveland Indians had now found a new outlet for his love of stealing from unsuspecting opponents on the athletic field. Baseball was now blessed with an outstanding new base-running champ who might some day soon challenge even the immortals of the game like Cobb, Brock, and Henderson.

KENNY LOFTON

BORN: May 31, 1967, East Chicago, Indiana.

CAREER: 1991–

TEAMS: Houston Astros, Cleveland Indians.

POSITION: Outfielder.

AWARDS AND ACHIEVEMENTS: American League Stolen Base
Champion, 1992–1994.

American League Leader in Base Hits, 1994.

Gold Glove Outfielder, 1993.

Before he was a star outfielder in the major leagues, Lofton had
been noticed by NBA scouts who watched him play basketball for
the University of Arizona Wildcats.

JOE MORGAN

Joe Morgan, along with Pete Rose, Tony Peréz, and Johnny Bench, led the Cincinnati Reds to World Series victories two years in a row.

THE CINCINNATI REDS TEAM OF 1975–1976 was one of the most powerful and star-studded in baseball history. This team was the first National League club to win back-to-back world titles since the New York Giants a half-century earlier in 1921 and 1922. Its lineup featured baseball's all-time hits leader, Pete Rose. Another star performer was the greatest Latin American slugger of them all, Tony Peréz, the career leader in home runs (tied with Orlando Cepeda) among Latin-American stars. Baseball's greatest catcher of the modern era, Johnny Bench, was in that lineup as well. Joe Morgan was sometimes overshadowed in the eyes of Cincinnati fans. But his teammates never lost sight of the true value Morgan brought to this exceptional team. His defense was one key to the club's endless victories. His bat and exceptional base-running skills were perhaps an even greater factor in the championship drive of the powerhouse Reds known as the Big Red Machine.

Few players ever enjoyed a season like the one Morgan celebrated in 1975. He led the league in walks, batted .327, hit 17 homers, just missed knocking in 100 runs, and also stole 67 bases. He was naturally the league's Most Valuable Player and sparked his Cincinnati team into the World Series against the Boston Red Sox. It was Morgan, of course, who was in the middle of much of that excitement. In game three, "Little Joe" knocked in the winning run with a single in the tenth. In game four, he failed to deliver and made the last out in a game that Boston hung on to win. In game seven, however, his single in the top of the ninth gave the Reds their first World Championship since 1940.

But it was in game five, after failing to deliver a day

earlier, that Joe Morgan used his special base-running skills to inspire a Cincinnati win and turn the series in favor of the Reds. Morgan had reached base in the sixth inning of a tight game and worried the Boston pitcher with his threat to steal. He would next draw an incredible 16 pickoff throws from the worried pitcher. By then the pitcher's concentration was broken. Bench singled and Peréz pounded out a three-run homer. Morgan had done the job of any base-stealing wizard. He had rattled an opposing pitcher and forced a game-deciding mistake.

Joe Morgan was a true rarity in baseball history. He was a small, agile, and speedy middle infielder who also possessed a slugger's power and a long-legged outfielder's graceful base-running speed. Few in the history of the game have better combined base-running agility, defensive skills, and slugging prowess as well. Joe Morgan was a feared hitter who drew more bases on balls than any other hitter in all of baseball history except for Ted Williams and Babe Ruth. He also had 2,517 base hits. Morgan ranks ninth all-time on the base stealers list. He topped fifty in a single season on several occasions. His best performances always came in the Reds' championship years. It is easy to see why Joe Morgan is only the second baseman ever to win consecutive league Most Valuable Player awards.

Joe Morgan was also unique in another way. For here was one of the smallest number-three hitters of the modern era at only 5 feet 7 inches and 150 pounds. Despite his size Morgan pounded 268 homers, more than anyone else among baseball's greatest base stealers. If there is indeed such a thing as a triple-threat star in baseball, then the model would have to be Joe Morgan. No one else combined base running, slugging, and fielding better than this Hall-of-Famer who many veteran baseball watchers believe was the greatest second baseman of all time.

JOE MORGAN

BORN: September 19, 1943, Bonham, Texas.

CAREER: 1963–1984.

TEAMS: Houston Astros, Cincinnati Reds, San Francisco Giants, Philadelphia Phillies, Oakland Athletics.

POSITION: Second Baseman.

AWARDS AND ACHIEVEMENTS: National League Most Valuable Player, 1975–1976.

Gold Glove Second Baseman, 1973–1977.

National League Leader in Runs Scored, 1972.

National League Leader in Triples, 1971.

Baseball Hall of Fame, Elected 1990.

A triple threat, Joe Morgan combined base running, slugging, and fielding to make him one of the greatest second basemen of all time.

TIM RAINES

AN IMPORTANT YET LARGELY UNNOTICED milestone event occurred in Chicago's Comiskey Park on August 12, 1993. Veteran outfielder Tim "Rock" Raines led off the game between the home team White Sox and visiting Kansas City Royals with a long home run. This was not just any homer, however, for with his roundtripper, Raines had also banged out the 2,000th base hit of his successful major league career. Nearly two hundred batters in big league history had already reached this milestone, but only three others had ever achieved what Raines had now accomplished. For in addition to his 2,000 base hits, Raines had also now recorded other impressive milestone marks—500 or more stolen bases, 100 home runs, 1,000 runs scored, and 100 or more triples. Only Lou Brock, Ty Cobb, and Honus Wagner among all the immortals of the game had preceded Raines with this rare collection of milestone marks. Three weeks later when he walked for the 1,000th time in his career, Raines joined Ty Cobb alone as players who could add 1,000 bases on balls to the rare mix.

Rock Raines has a nickname that suggests both bulging muscles and superior physical strength. Most of Raines's muscles are apparently found in his legs; they have stolen 764 bases during a 16-year major league career split between the National League Montreal Expos and the American League Chicago White Sox. Six times Raines has recorded a batting average of better than .300, and six times he has pounded out 175 or more hits in a major league season. He even has some pop in his bat and hits for occasional power, recording double figures in home runs on six different occasions. But

TIM RAINES

Not only has Tim Raines stolen nearly 800 bases in his career, he has slugged over 2,000 base hits, 100 home runs, 100 triples, and scored over 1,000 runs.

the legacy of Tim Raines as a baseball star is one of speed—in the outfield and on the bases.

Nowhere was Raines more able to demonstrate his speed than in his early days in the National League. The young Raines exploded on the National League scene in 1981 when he stole 71 bases, the most steals ever recorded by an untried rookie during more than a century of major league play. This rookie total was all the more amazing since the Montreal speedster performed in only 88 games, during a season that was cut nearly in half by a long mid-year players' union strike. For the next three straight seasons, Raines would again pace the National League in stolen bases, and for two years after that he would also again steal 70 bases each season. Raines' 634 steals in the National League still stands as the seventh highest total in modern senior circuit history.

Today, Tim Raines no longer runs the bases and patrols the outfield for the Montreal team. Instead, he performs similar duties for the American League Chicago White Sox. Despite his advancing age, Raines is still used by the White Sox club as a leadoff batter, a position in the lineup usually reserved for a speedy and selective batsman. The batsman will work his way around the bases and then tantalize opposing pitchers from the base paths while more powerful sluggers follow him to the plate.

No matter what Raines accomplishes for the remainder of his career in the American League, he has already left his lasting mark on baseball as one of the game's most daring base runners of the modern age. The Chicago outfielder now stands fourth on the list of all-time twentieth-century base stealers with 764, ranking behind only Rickey Henderson, Lou Brock, and Ty Cobb. And there is still enough speed in those legs to move Raines even further ahead of those who might someday challenge his own lofty ranking.

TIM RAINES

BORN: September 16, 1959, Sanford, Florida.

CAREER: 1979–

TEAMS: Montreal Expos, Chicago White Sox.

POSITION: Outfielder.

AWARDS AND ACHIEVEMENTS: National League Stolen Base Champion,
1981–1984.

National League Leader in Runs Scored, 1983, 1987.

National League Batting Champion, 1986.

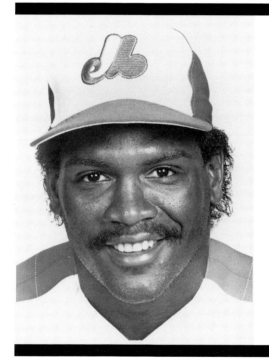

"Rock" Raines has played well consistently during his sixteen year career in the major leagues.

NSIDE

BASEBA

ry • 35c

is

JACKIE ROBINSON

Many consider Jackie Robinson's steal of home in the opening game of the 1955 World Series the most exciting play in baseball history.

JACKIE ROBINSON

THE OPENING GAME OF THE 1955 World Series between Brooklyn and New York was a closely contested hitters' game. The heated rivals were battling each other for baseball's world championship for the fifth time in nine years. Emotions ran high as they always did when these city rivals met in what came to be known as their "subway-series" matchups. Both teams scored twice in the second inning and once more in the third frame. Then Joe Collins, the Yankees' slugging first baseman, smacked two long homers. Suddenly the National League team felt yet another chance slipping away against the powerhouse Yankees who always seemed to best them in these dramatic Fall Classic battles.

But Brooklyn fought back, as this brave Brooklyn Dodgers team did so often. In the eighth inning, speedster Jackie Robinson reached third and immediately began his terrorizing dance away from the bag. Some of the New York sportswriters had earlier called the veteran Robinson "that old gray fatman" because he was now late in his career and carrying extra weight and silver hair.[1] Now Robinson, the first African American to play in the major leagues in the twentieth century, would show his critics that there was still speed in his legs as he dashed for the plate in a successful surprise steal of home. The Yankees ace lefty pitcher Whitey Ford had indeed been taken by surprise by Robinson's daring move and delivered to the plate a split second too late. When Robinson broke for home plate, he had taken charge of the game. His steal brought the Brooklyn team back to within one run of the lead.

Jackie Robinson had once again inspired his teammates

as he had done so many times before. His run in that first game of the 1955 World Series was not enough to bring a Brooklyn victory. It had, nonetheless, instilled a new life in the Dodgers who now took a clue from their emotional leader. The Brooklyn team soon battled back for a thrilling seven-game triumph and in the process earned their first and only world championship during the team's half-century stay in Brooklyn. The aging Robinson would register only four hits and bat a weak .182 during what would be his next-to-last World Series appearance. But no Dodger had played a more important role in Brooklyn's dramatic championship victory than team leader Jackie Robinson, who had launched the championship drive with his daring steal of home.

Robinson also had more magic in store for the Yankees that autumn. The real turning point of the series came perhaps in the third game. Robinson had again reached third base, and with the bases now loaded, he played his cat and mouse game with Yankee hurler Bob Turley. Robinson's threats toward home plate distracted the Yankee pitcher, who suddenly lost sight of the strike zone with his deliveries and thus walked Junior Gilliam on four straight pitches. The lead run had been walked home, and the Dodgers again cruised to an important victory. Even when he didn't steal a base, Robinson nonetheless had a way of pressuring pitchers into giving up the crucial run when it was most needed.

Many old-timers still consider a Jackie Robinson steal of home plate to be the most exciting play ever witnessed on a baseball diamond. Hall-of-Fame outfielder Ralph Kiner of the Pittsburgh Pirates best summarized Robinson's impact on opposing ballclubs. "He is the only player I ever saw," recalled Kiner, "who could turn a game around completely by himself."[2] This was the kind of excitement Robinson generated with his dramatic steal of home plate in the greatest World Series in Brooklyn baseball history.

JACKIE ROBINSON

BORN: January 31, 1919, Cairo, Georgia.

DIED: October 24, 1972, Stanford, Connecticut.

CAREER: 1947–1956.

TEAM: Brooklyn Dodgers.

POSITION: Infielder and Outfielder.

AWARDS AND ACHIEVEMENTS: National League Rookie of the Year, 1947.

National League Most Valuable Player, 1949.

National League Batting Champion, 1949.

National League Stolen Base Champion, 1947, 1949.

National League Leader in Fielding Percentage for Second Basemen, 1948, 1950–1951.

Baseball Hall of Fame, Elected 1962.

The excitement that Jackie Robinson brought to the game helped the Brooklyn Dodgers win their only world championship.

MAURY WILLS

SOME STAR BALLPLAYERS ARE KNOWN for their year-in and year-out consistency. Year after year these stars pound out base hits, blast home runs, or—in the case of pitchers—mystify opposing hitters and pile up victories with endless regularity. A small handful of the game's memorable stars, however, are rare one-season wonders. These overnight sensations flash onto the scene for a brilliant season or two. Then they suddenly fade just as rapidly as they arrived, and fans are left to wonder how their heroes could be so good one summer and so mediocre the next.

Among baseball's brief comets, none flashed more brightly or burned out more rapidly than Maury Wills. He was the speedster who manned shortstop for the weak-hitting Los Angeles Dodgers of the early 1960s. For Maury Wills the summer of 1962 was a dream season indeed. Wills had already been the base-stealing champion in the National League for two years when the 1962 season arrived. But he had hardly been a recognized star, and his weak-hitting Dodgers were not considered to be one of the more glamorous National League teams. Then suddenly, Wills's base-stealing proficiency was enough to place the Dodgers team—with its solid pitching and tight defense—straight into the middle of a tight pennant race with the rival San Francisco Giants. Wills was so skilled on the bases that particular summer that he was soon approaching Ty Cobb's single-season record of 96 steals, which had stood unchallenged for nearly half a century.

As the thrilling pennant race drew to a close, the powerhouse Giants would nip the light-hitting Dodgers at the wire

Maury Wills was the first man to steal over one hundred bases in a single season.

in a dramatic play off for the National League championship. But while Wills's Dodgers fell short of overtaking the Giants, the speedster himself flew by Cobb's record in the final weeks of the summer, becoming the first man ever to steal 100 bases in a single season. The Dodgers wizard of the base paths not only smashed Cobb's previous record total but also proved far more efficient than Cobb at base thievery as well.[1] Wills had been thrown out only 13 times all summer, but Cobb failed on 38 attempts during his own record-setting season back in 1915.

It was Wills's base stealing and league-leading number of triples in that remarkable summer of 1962 that brought the Dodgers shortstop his coveted award as the league's Most Valuable Player. Wills did not lead the National League that year in any other single important department. After the miracle year of 1962, baseball's base-stealing wizard would remain a serious thorn in the side of National League pitchers for a few more years. For three more seasons, he would remain the best in the league at his specialty, but his success ratio at stealing began to fall off dramatically. Only four seasons after his single remarkable summer, Wills had slipped enough for the Dodgers to trade him away to the Pittsburgh Pirates where his career began a rapid fall from the limelight. Never again would Maury Wills be the league's top base-stealing threat. The magic mastery that Wills briefly owned over league pitchers and catchers had suddenly disappeared.

When it comes to the game's great base runners, Maury Wills was indeed a wonder. He would never be known for consistency like Cobb, Aparicio, or Rickey Henderson. His influence on the game would not be enjoyed for very long. But Maury Wills enjoyed great fame as baseball's king of the stolen base.

MAURY WILLS

BIRTHDATE: October 2, 1932, Washington, D.C.

CAREER: 1959–1972.

TEAMS: Los Angeles Dodgers, Pittsburgh Pirates, Montreal Expos.

POSITION: Shortstop and Third Baseman.

AWARDS AND ACHIEVEMENTS: National League Most Valuable Player,
1962.

National League Stolen Base Champion, 1960–1965.

Gold Glove Shortstop, 1961–1962.

National League Leader in Triples, 1962.

In 1962, Wills was voted the league's Most Valuable Player for his
incredible base-stealing ability.

BASEBALL'S GREAT BASE STEALERS COMPARED

Player	Career Stolen Bases	Years Led League	Steals per Season	Best Single Season total
RICKEY HENDERSON	1,117	11	70	130 (1982)
LOU BROCK	938	8	52	118 (1974)
TY COBB	891	6	39	96 (1915)
TIM RAINES	764	4	55	90 (1983)
EDDIE COLLINS	744	4	35	81 (1910)
JOE MORGAN	689	0	36	67 (1973, 1975)
MAURY WILLS	586	6	42	104 (1962)
LUÍS APARICIO	506	9	28	57 (1964)
JACKIE ROBINSON	197	2	20	37 (1949)
KENNY LOFTON	198	3	66	70 (1993)

NOTES BY CHAPTER

Luís Aparicio
1. Michael Gershman, "The 100 Greatest Players," *Total Baseball: The Ultimate Encyclopedia of Baseball*, third ed., edited by John Thorn and Pete Palmer (New York: HarperCollins, 1993), p. 158.

Lou Brock
No notes.

Ty Cobb
1. Norman L. Macht, *Ty Cobb* (Philadelphia and London: Chelsea House, 1993), pp. 35–37.
2. Jack Kavanagh, *Walter Johnson* (Philadelphia and London: Chelsea House, 1992), p. 28.

Eddie Collins
No notes.

Rickey Henderson
1. Mike Shatzkin, ed., *The Ballplayers: Baseball's Ultimate Biographical Reference* (New York: Morrow, 1990), p. 462.
2. Rickey Henderson and John Shea, *Off Base: Confessions of a Thief* (New York: HarperCollins, 1992), p. 117.

Kenny Lofton
No notes.

Joe Morgan
No notes.

Tim Raines
No notes.

Jackie Robinson
1. Harvey Frommer, *Jackie Robinson* (New York: Franklin Watts, 1984), p. 81.
2. John Grabowski, *Jackie Robinson* (Philadelphia and London: Chelsea House, 1992), pp. 35–36.

Maury Wills
1. Mike Shatzkin, ed., *The Ballplayers: Baseball's Ultimate Biographical Reference* (New York: Morrow, 1990), p. 1183.

INDEX